Habitat Destruction

by Helen Orme

Consultant: Terry Jennings, Ph.D.
Educational Consultant

BEARPORT
PUBLISHING

New York, New York

Credits

Cover and Title Page, © Peter Lilja/age fotostock/SuperStock; Credit Page, © Sam D Cruz/Shutterstock; 4, © Jan Martin Will/Shutterstock; 4–5, © LWPhotography/Shutterstock; 7, © Keith Wood/Corbis Premium RF/Alamy; 8, © Wesley Aston/Shutterstock; 8–9, © Phil Degginger/Alamy; 10–11, © Tyler Olson/Shutterstock; 11, © Galina Barskaya/Shutterstock; 12, © Michel Stevelmans/Shutterstock; 12–13, © Photodisc/SuperStock; 14–15, © Creatas/SuperStock; 15, © Sergei Chumakov/Shutterstock; 16–17, © Mostovyi Sergii Igorevich/Shutterstock; 18–19, © Bart Everett/Shutterstock; 19, © Armin Rose/Shutterstock; 20, © Pete Oxford/Nature Picture Library; 21, © Morley Read/iStockphoto; 22–23, © Kimberly Hall/Shutterstock; 23, © Ammon Andrew Cogdill/Shutterstock; 24, © Hannamariah/Shutterstock; 25, © Elena Kalistratova/Shutterstock; 26, © Micheline Pelletier/Corbis; 27, © NHPA/A.N.T. PHOTO LIBRARY; 28, © Morozova Tatyana/Shutterstock; 29T, © Rostislav Glinsky/Shutterstock; 29B, © Mayskyphoto/Shutterstock; 30, © Kenneth V. Pilon/Shutterstock.

Every effort has been made to trace the copyright holders, and we apologize in advance for any unintentional omissions. We would be pleased to insert the appropriate acknowledgments in any subsequent edition of this publication.

The Earth in Danger series is printed on recycled paper.

Library of Congress Cataloging-in-Publication Data

Orme, Helen.
 Habitat destruction / by Helen Orme.
  p. cm. — (Earth in danger)
 Includes index.
 ISBN-13: 978-1-59716-725-3 (library binding)
 ISBN-10: 1-59716-725-8 (library binding)
 1. Habitat (Ecology) — Juvenile literature. 2. Nature— Effect of human beings on— Juvenile literature. 3. Habitat conservation— Juvenile literature. 4. Conservation of natural resources— Juvenile literature. I. Title.

 QH541.14.O76 2009
 577.27—dc22
                        2008022224

Contents

What Is a Habitat? .4

Habitats in Danger. 6

Land for Living. .8

Land for Farming 10

Mining the Land. 12

Using Too Much Water 14

Water Pollution. 16

Air Pollution 18

Rain Forests at Risk 20

Protecting the Planet. 22

Just the Facts. 24

How to Help 30

Learn More Online. 30

Glossary 31

Index 32

Read More 32

What Is a Habitat?

A habitat is a place in nature where living things make their home. Forests, mountains, deserts, grasslands, and oceans are habitats for plants and animals. All living things get food, water, and everything else they need to survive from these places.

Different kinds of plants and animals need different kinds of habitats. For example, a polar bear needs to live in a cold, icy place. It couldn't survive in a hot, dry desert. If its habitat is damaged or destroyed, the bear can't just move somewhere else. It may die out and become **extinct**.

A polar bear's icy home

Every animal has **adapted** to its own habitat. For example, ducks live in rivers and ponds. Their feet are webbed so they can move quickly through water.

Habitats in Danger

Who could destroy a habitat? The answer is people.

People damage habitats to get the **natural resources** they need from Earth. They clear land to plant **crops** for food, cut down forests to get wood for building homes, and dig into the ground to get oil and coal for **fuel**.

Long ago, there were fewer people on the planet than there are now. People could get what they needed from Earth without destroying many habitats. Today, the world's **population** is growing very quickly and lots of resources are needed. This means that more habitats are being destroyed. There are now fewer and fewer places where wildlife can survive.

The planet's population is increasing very quickly. In 1950, there were 2.5 billion people in the world. By 2050, there will be more than 9 billion people.

A new home being built

Land for Living

One of the resources people need most from the earth is land to live on. Picture a big city. Think about what was there before it was built. The land was probably covered with trees or grasses. It was a habitat for plants and animals. Now the land is covered by streets, sidewalks, and buildings. There are few places for wildlife to live.

As the population continues to grow, cities and towns get bigger and more habitats disappear. This is why wild animals such as deer or bears are sometimes seen in parks or even in people's backyards. They have nowhere else to go to find the food and other things they need to survive.

New York City, pictured below, is the most populated city in the United States. As of 2007, more than 8 million people live there. Mumbai, India, is one of the most populated cities in the world, with more than 13 million people.

Land for Farming

People also need land for growing food. Once, small farms could grow enough crops and raise enough animals to feed the world's population. Now, with the ever increasing number of people on the planet, more food must be grown. This means that bigger farms are needed. To make room for them, more grasslands have to be cleared and more forests have to be cut down. Sometimes swamps and marshes also have to be drained.

Many farmers use **chemical fertilizers** to make crops grow more quickly. These chemicals drain into ponds and streams. They **pollute** the water that animals and people need to survive. Some farmers also use **pesticides** to kill insects that damage crops. Pesticides **endanger** birds and other animals that eat the poisoned insects.

Fish killed by pollution

Mining the Land

People also dig into the land to get useful materials. This is called **mining**.

One of the most important materials that people mine is iron ore. Ore is needed to produce steel for cars, trains, bridges, and tall buildings. People also dig into the earth to get fuels such as oil, gas, and coal. They need these sources of energy to heat buildings, run cars, and produce electricity.

It's impossible to mine without damaging habitats and killing living things. Sometimes mining companies dig huge holes in the land. Other times they use **explosives** to blow away entire mountaintops.

A machine that digs for coal

At this mine, people dig for copper.

Strip mining is used to mine coal that is near Earth's surface. Huge power shovels remove the soil and rocks that cover the coal. Then the coal is shoveled out of the ground and an area of damaged land is left behind. More than two million acres (809,371 hectares) of land have been strip mined in the United States.

Using Too Much Water

Using land isn't the only way people damage and destroy habitats. Another way is by using too much water. All living things need water to survive. Plants and animals get water from rivers, lakes, and the soil that are part of their habitats.

Are people using too much water? Yes. The problem is that people don't use water just for drinking and washing. They also use it for watering crops and for producing things such as paper, chemicals, and electricity. Rain can't replace all the water that's being used. So many rivers and lakes are beginning to dry up.

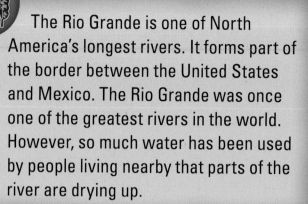

The Rio Grande is one of North America's longest rivers. It forms part of the border between the United States and Mexico. The Rio Grande was once one of the greatest rivers in the world. However, so much water has been used by people living nearby that parts of the river are drying up.

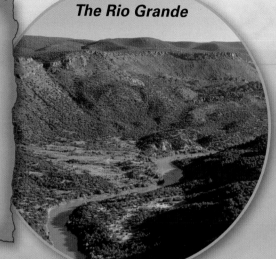

The Rio Grande

Snake River in Wyoming

Water Pollution

People also damage habitats by causing water pollution. Much of the water pollution comes from factories, which make goods such as cars, clothing, shoes, refrigerators, computers, and books.

Factories use chemicals to produce plastics, rubber, cloth, and other materials. Then they have to get rid of the chemicals. Sometimes, factories dump used chemicals into rivers, streams, and oceans. Many of them are harmful to plants and animals. The chemicals pollute the water, killing some of the living things in it. Also, animals that live on land get sick or die from drinking the polluted water.

Cars can also cause water pollution. Oil from cars can leak onto roadways. Rain washes the oil into rivers, which carry it into the ocean. Oil in ocean waters harms fish, otters, birds, and other sea life.

A factory on a river

Air Pollution

Air pollution is caused by fuels, such as gas, oil, and coal, which are burned by machines in factories, cars and trucks, and power plants. These fuels release **carbon dioxide** and other gases into the air when they burn. Carbon dioxide is a gas that traps the sun's heat in Earth's **atmosphere**.

Carbon dioxide is already a natural part of air. It keeps the planet warm enough for people, plants, and animals to survive. However, adding more carbon dioxide to the air is making the planet too warm. Scientists call this change **global warming**.

Why is global warming a problem? Living things need a particular **climate** to survive in their habitats. Many plant and animal **species** will die out if their habitats become warmer.

Scientists say that temperatures on Earth have gone up about 1°F (0.6°C) during the last 100 years. They believe that temperatures could go up as much as 11°F (6°C) in the next 100 years.

Warmer temperatures are melting ice at the North Pole and the South Pole.

Rain Forests at Risk

All habitats on Earth are important. The tropical rain forest, however, is a special habitat. What are tropical rain forests? What makes them so special?

Tropical rain forests are thick forests full of tall trees. These forests grow near the **equator**. The climate is always hot and rainy there. Rain forests are special because they're home to more kinds of plants and animals than all the other habitats on Earth put together.

Rain forest habitats are at risk because people are cutting down the trees. They use the **timber** for making furniture. They use the land for farming and building roads. Some scientists think that more than 100 rain forest animal species are becoming extinct every day because they're losing their habitat.

The fossa from Madagascar, an African country, is just one of the many rain forest animals that's in danger of becoming extinct.

Cutting down rain forests increases global warming. Trees and other plants **absorb** carbon dioxide from the air. Rain forests are very large, so they absorb a huge amount of this gas.

A tropical rain forest

Protecting the Planet

Many of the things that people do in their everyday lives are harming habitats. Scientists are trying to find ways to protect habitats and still get the resources that people need.

One of their ideas is to grow crops that are good for the soil. Peanuts, soybeans, and peas are natural fertilizers. By growing these crops, farmers can reduce the amount of chemical fertilizers they use to grow other crops.

Scientists and others also think that people should stop using fuels that release carbon dioxide into the air. Other sources of power such as wind, water, and the sun are good ways to get energy without damaging the **environment**.

A soybean field

Trees in Nicaragua

Scientists also believe that planting trees is another way to protect habitats. For example, in Nicaragua, a country in Central America, farmers are being paid to plant trees on land where forests have been cut down. Planting new forests will keep 150,000 tons (136,078 metric tons) of carbon dioxide out of the air. The new forests will also provide a habitat for wildlife.

More Tropical Rain Forest Facts

Here are some interesting facts about tropical rain forests.

- About 10 million species of plants and animals live on Earth. More than half of those species live in tropical rain forests.

- Rain forests are full of plants that may be useful for curing deadly diseases, such as cancer.

- Trees give off the oxygen we need to breathe. Almost half of the world's oxygen is produced in rain forests.

- People live in tropical rain forests. When the forests are cut down, these people lose their homes.

This map shows Earth's major tropical rain forests.

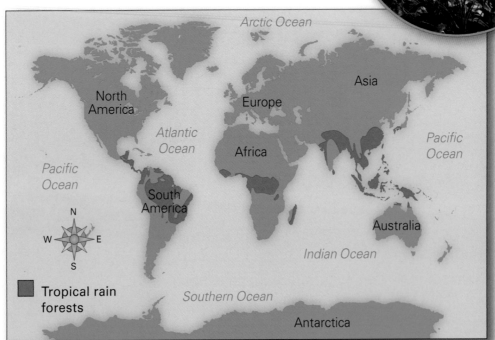

Friendly Food

Some foods can be produced with less damage to habitats than others. Help save habitats by carefully choosing what foods to eat.

- Buy foods that are labeled "organic." This means that they're grown without using chemical fertilizers or pesticides, which are harmful to the environment.

- Eat more fruits, vegetables, and grains. Not only are they healthier than meat, but growing them is less damaging to habitats than raising cattle and other farm animals.

- Buy fish that are line-caught. "Line-caught" fish are taken from the sea in low numbers. This way, fish populations will not go down to the point where there are not enough fish to reproduce.

Trees for Africa

In 1976, a woman in Africa named Wangari Maathai was worried that forests in Africa were disappearing. She encouraged women to plant trees on their farms.

- Since then, women in Africa have planted more than 30 million trees.
- Wangari Maathai's work is known as the Green Belt Movement.
- In 2004, she won the Nobel Peace Prize for her work. She was the first woman from Africa to receive this honor.

Wangari Maathai

Invasive Species

A habitat can be damaged by species of animals or plants that don't belong there. Such species are called **invasives**. People sometimes bring invasive species into a habitat.

- Hundred of years ago, there were no rabbits in Australia. In 1859, a farmer in Australia decided he wanted to hunt rabbits. So he brought 24 wild rabbits from Europe. Within 10 years, Australia had more than 2 million rabbits!

- The rabbits ate so many plants that some species became extinct. Other animals that depended on these plants for food became endangered.

- Now governments are being very careful to not allow invasive plants and animals into their countries.

Coral Reefs

Coral reefs are formed by tiny sea animals called polyps. Many kinds of fish and other sea animals live in and around coral reefs. They are among the world's most beautiful habitats. However, they are in danger.

- Coral reefs can be damaged by water pollution or destroyed by underwater mining.

- Divers like to explore coral reefs. Sometimes they damage the reefs by touching them or standing on them. The divers' boats can also harm the reefs.

- Global warming is raising water temperatures. This kills the tiny sea animals that form coral reefs.

Wildlife Vacations

Many people love to travel to see wildlife in different parts of the world. Increased travel can damage habitats.

- Airplanes burn fuel that increases global warming.

- When air travel increases, new airports need to be built, causing habitats to be damaged and destroyed.

- Tourists need hotels to stay in. Hotels use lots of power and water.

- Sometimes tourists are not careful when they visit foreign habitats. They leave behind garbage or take away things such as endangered plants or animals.

How to Help

Everyone needs to get involved to help prevent habitat destruction. Here are some things to do:

- Encourage family members to walk or ride bicycles instead of using a car. Cars release carbon dioxide into the air. Walking and cycling do not.

- Recycle all paper. Wood from trees is used in making paper, so saving paper means saving trees.

- Plant a tree.

- Don't waste electricity. Power plants burn coal or oil to make electricity, and this pollutes the air.

- Don't waste water. Living things depend on it.

- Ask family members not to use chemical fertilizers and pesticides in the garden.

- Learn about protecting habitats. Then tell others what you've learned.

- Join an organization such as the World Wildlife Fund (www. worldwildlife.org) that supports endangered habitats.

Learn More Online

To learn more about habitat destruction, visit
www.bearportpublishing.com/EarthinDanger

Glossary

absorb (ab-ZORB) to soak up something

adapted (uh-DAP-tid) changed over time to be fit for the environment

atmosphere (AT-muhss-fihr) the air, or mixture of gases, that surround Earth

carbon dioxide (KAR-buhn dye-OK-side) a colorless and odorless gas given off when things decay or are burned

chemical (KEM-uh-kuhl) a man-made substance that can sometimes be harmful to living things

climate (KLYE-mit) the typical weather in a place

crops (KROPS) plants that are grown and gathered, often for food

endanger (en-DAYN-jur) to put into a dangerous situation

environment (en-VYE-ruhn-muhnt) the plants, animals, and weather in a place

equator (i-KWAY-tur) the imaginary line halfway between the North Pole and South Pole that runs around the middle of Earth

explosives (ek-SPLOH-sivz) things that blow up

extinct (ek-STINGKT) when a kind of plant or animal has died out; no more of its kind is living anywhere in the world

fertilizers (FUR-tuh-lye-zerz) substances added to soil to make crops grow

fuel (FYOO-uhl) something that is used as a source of energy or heat, such as gasoline

global warming (GLOHB-uhl WORM-ing) the gradual heating up of Earth caused by greenhouse gases trapping heat from the sun in Earth's atmosphere

invasives (in-VAY-sivz) plants or animals that have been moved from their habitat into another habitat in which they do not naturally belong

mining (MINE-ing) digging up minerals that are underground

natural resources (NACH-ur-uhl REE-sorss-iz) materials found in nature that people use or need

pesticides (PESS-tuh-*sidez*) poisonous chemicals used to kill insects and other pests

pollute (puh-LOOT) to release harmful substances into the environment

population (*pop*-yuh-LAY-shuhn) the total number of people who live in an area

species (SPEE-sheez) groups that animals are divided into, according to similar characteristics; members of the same species can have offspring together

timber (TIM-buhr) wood used for building

Index

air 18, 21, 23, 30

animals 4–5, 8, 10–11, 14, 16, 18, 20, 24, 27, 28–29

carbon dioxide 18, 21, 22–23, 30

chemicals 11, 14, 16, 22, 25, 30

coal 6, 12–13, 18, 30

coral reefs 28

crops 6, 10–11, 14, 22

electricity 12, 14, 30

factories 16, 18

farming 10–11, 20, 22–23, 25, 26

food 4, 6, 8, 10, 25, 27

fuel 6, 12, 18, 22, 29

gas 12, 18, 21

global warming 18, 21, 28–29

habitats 4–5, 6, 8, 12, 14, 16, 18, 20, 22–23, 25, 27, 28–29, 30

invasive species 27

land 6, 8, 10, 12–13, 14, 16, 20, 23

Maathai, Wangari 26

mining 12–13

oceans 4, 16–17

oil 6, 12, 17, 18, 30

plants 4, 8, 14, 16, 18, 20–21, 24, 27, 29

pollution 11, 16–17, 18

population 6, 8–9, 10, 25

rain forests 20–21, 24

rivers 5, 14–15, 16–17

streams 11, 16

trees 8, 20–21, 23, 24, 26, 30

water 4–5, 11, 14–15, 16–17, 22, 28–29, 30

wildlife 6, 8, 23, 29

Read More

Burnie, David, and Tony Juniper. *Endangered Planet.* Boston: Kingfisher (2004).

Harlow, Rosie, and Sally Morgan. *Nature in Danger.* New York: Kingfisher (2001).